D0807389

MOHAWK
TRAIL

Also by Beth Brant:

A Gathering of Spirit (ed.)

MOHAWK TRAIL

by BETH BRANT
(Degonwadonti)

Firebrand
Books
Ithaca, New York 14850

Selections from *Mohawk Trail* have appeared previously in the following books and periodicals: *Bearing Witness/Sobreviviendo* (Calyx), *Corridors, A Gathering of Spirit* (Sinister Wisdom), *Greenfield Review, Ikon, Live Writers!, A Nation Within* (Outrigger Publishers), *New Lesbian Writing* (Grey Fox Press), *Plainswoman, Sinister Wisdom, Songs from This Earth on Turtle's Back* (Greenfield Review Press), and *13th Moon.*

Cover and book design by Mary A. Scott

The cover is based on a quilt design, *Mohawk Trail*, created by the author's grandmother, Margaret Brant, almost fifty years ago.

Typesetting by Martha J. Waters

Printed in the United States by McNaughton & Gunn, Inc.

Library of Congress Cataloging in Publication Data

Brant, Beth, 1941-
  Mohawk trail.

  1. Mohawk Indians--Literary collections. I. Title.
PR 9199.3.B687M6 1985   818'.5409   85-3265
ISBN 0-932379-03-6
ISBN 0-932379-02-8 (pbk.)

For my families. And for Jimmy,
who would have loved this book.

Acknowledgments

When I knew *Mohawk Trail* was going to be a reality and not a dream, I made a mental list of all the people who helped me get to this point. The mental list was put on paper, the paper turned into pages, and I realized that I could not possibly name everyone who means so much to me. But there are names who must *must* go on the page. It's my giveaway to them.

Michelle Cliff, Mary Moran, Chrystos, Gloria Anzaldúa, Adrienne Rich, Elaine Hall, Barbara Cameron, Catherine Daligga, Terri Meyette, Kate Shanley, Janice Gould, Doris Seale, Awiakta, and the women at Women's Voices—1982, especially Marcy Alancraig, Sheila Hallet, and Paula Ross.

Briarcombe Foundation, where many of the Songs were written.

My mom and dad I want to thank for giving me just the right blend of Indian spirit and Irish/Scots practicality.

Thank you Betsey Beaven and Ann Brooks for the gifts of money, and for the greater gift—faith.

Denise Dorsz, lover and mate of eight years, thank you for not asking me to go out and get a steady job. Thank you for filling me with blessings.

And thank you Nancy Bereano for believing in my politics, my language, my work.

Contents

Ride the Turtle's Back

A woman grows hard and skinny.
She squeezes into small corners.
Her quick eyes uncover dust and cobwebs.
She reaches out
for flint and sparks fly in the air.
Flames turned loose on fields
burn down to bare seeds
we planted deep.

The corn is white and sweet.
Under its pale, perfect kernels
a rotting cob is betrayal.
It lies in our bloated stomachs.

I lie in Grandmother's bed
and dream the earth into a turtle.
She carries us slowly across the universe.
The sun warms us.
At night the stars do tricks.
The moon caresses us.

We are listening for the sounds of food.

Mother is giving birth, Grandmother says.
Corn whispers.
The earth groans with labor
turning corn yellow in the sun.

I lie in Grandmother's bed.

We listen.

Part One
NATIVE ORIGIN

Native Origin

The old women are gathered in the Longhouse. First, the ritual kissing on the cheeks, the eyes, the lips, the top of the head; that spot where the hair parts in the middle like a wild river through a canyon.

A Grandmother sets the pot over the fire that has never gone out. To let the flames die is a taboo, a break of trust. The acorn shells have been roasted the night before. Grandmother pours the boiling water over the shells. An aroma rises and combines with the smell of wood smoke, sweat, and the sharp-sweet odor of blood.

The acorn coffee steeps and grows strong and dark. The old women sit patiently in a circle, not speaking. Each set of eyes stares sharply into the air or the fire. Occasionally, a sigh is let loose from open mouth. A Grandmother has a twitch in the corner of her eye. She rubs her nose, then smooths her hair.

The coffee is ready. Cups are brought from a wooden cupboard. Each woman is given the steaming brew. They blow on the swirling liquid, then slurp the drink into hungry mouths. It tastes good. Hot, dark, strong. A little bitter, but that is all to the good.

The women begin talking among themselves. They are together to perform a ceremony. Rituals of old women take time. There is no hurry.

The magic things are brought out from pockets and pouches.

A turtle rattle made from a she-turtle who was a companion of the woman's mother. It died the night she died, both of them ancient and tough. Now, the daughter shakes the rattle, and mother and she-turtle live again.

A bundle containing a feather from a hermit thrush. This is a holy feather. Of all the birds in the sky, hermit thrush is the one who flew to the Spirit World. It was there she learned her beautiful song. She is clever and hides from sight. To have her feather is great magic. The women pass the feather. They tickle each other's chins and ears. Giggles and laughter erupt in the dwelling.

Bundles of corn, kernels of red, yellow, black. These also are passed from wrinkled hand to dry palm. Each woman holds the corn in her hand for a while before giving it to her sister.

Leaves of Witch Hazel and Jewelweed. Dandelion roots for chewing. Pearly Everlasting for smoking. These things are given careful attention. Much talk is generated over the old ways of preparing these gifts.

A woman gives a smile and brings a cradleboard from behind her back. There is nodding of heads and laughter and long drawn-out "ahhhhhs." The cradleboard has a beaded back that a mother made in her ninth month. An old woman starts a song; the others join her:

Little baby
Little baby
Ride on Mother's back
Laugh, laugh
Life is good
Mother shields you
Mother shields you.

A Grandmother wipes her eyes, another holds her hands and kisses the lifelines.

Inside the cradleboard are bunches of moss taken from a menstrual house. This moss has staunched lakes of blood that generations of women have squeezed from their wombs.

The acorn drink is reheated and passed once more. A woman adds wood to the fire. She holds her arms out to the flames. Another woman comes behind her with a warm blanket. She wraps it around her friend and hugs her shoulders. They stand before the fire.

A pelt of fur is brought forth. It once belonged to a beaver. She was found one morning, frozen in the ice, her lodge unfinished. The beaver was thawed and skinned. The women worked the hide until it was soft and pliant. It was the right size to wrap a newborn in, or to comfort old women on cold nights.

A piece of flint. An eagle bone whistle. A hank of black hair, cut in mourning. These are examined with reverence.

The oldest Grandmother removes a pouch from around her neck. She opens it with rusty fingers. She spreads the contents in her lap. A fistful of dark earth.

It smells clean, fecund. The women inhale the odor. The metallic taste of iron is on their tongues, like a sting.

The oldest Grandmother scoops the earth back into her pouch. She tugs at the string. It closes. The pouch lies between her breasts, warming her skin. Her breasts are supple and soft for one so old. Not long ago, she nursed a sister back to health. A child drank from her and was healed of evil spirits that entered her as she lay innocent and dreaming.

The ceremony is over. The magic things are put in their places. The women kiss and touch each other's faces. They go out into the night. The moon and stars are parts of Sky Woman. She glows— never dimming, never retreating.

The Grandmothers gather inside the Longhouse. They tend the fire.

Mohawk Trail

There is a small body of water in Canada called the Bay of Quinte. Look for three pine trees gnarled and entwined together. Woodland Indians, they call the people who live here. This is a reserve of Mohawks, the People of the Flint. On this reserve lived a woman of the Turtle Clan. Her name was Eliza, and she had many children. Her daughters bore flower names—Pansy, Daisy, Ivy, and Margaret Rose.

Margaret grew up, married Joseph of the Wolf Clan. They had a son. He was Joseph, too. Eight children later, they moved to Detroit, America. More opportunities for Margaret's children. Grandpa Joseph took a mail-order course in drafting. He thought Detroit would educate his Turtle children. It did.

Joseph, the son, met a white woman. Her name is Hazel. Together, they made me. All of Margaret's children married white. So, the children of Margaret's children are different. Half-blood. "Half-breed," Uncle Doug used to tease. But he smiled as he said it. Uncle was a musician and played jazz. They called him Red. Every Christmas Eve, Uncle phoned us kids and pretended he was Santa. He asked, "Were you good little Indians or bad little Indians?" We, of course, would tell tales of our goodness to our mothers and grandmother. Uncle signed off with a "ho ho ho" and a shake of his turtle rattle. Uncle died from alcohol. He was buried in a shiny black suit, his rattle in his hands, and a beaded turtle around his neck.

Some of my aunts went to college. Grandma baked pies and bread for Grandpa to sell in the neighborhood. It helped to pay for the precious education. All of my aunts had skills, had jobs. Shirley became a dietician and cooked meals for kids in school. She was the first Indian in the state of Michigan to get that degree. She was very proud of what she had done for The People. Laura was a secretary. She received a plaque one year from her boss, proclaiming her speed at typing. Someone had painted a picture of an Indian in headdress typing furiously. Laura was supposed to laugh but she didn't. She quit instead. Hazel could do anything. She worked as a cook, as a clerk in a five and ten-cent store. She made jewelry out of shells and stones and sold them door to door. Hazel was the first divorcée in our family. It was thrilling to be the niece of a woman so bold. Elsie was a sickly girl. She didn't go to school and worked in a grocery store, minded women's children for extra money. She caught the streetcar in winter, bundled in Grandma's coat and wearing bits of warmth from her sisters' wardrobes. When she died, it wasn't from consumption or influenza. She died from eight children and cancer of the womb and breast. Colleen became a civil servant, serving the public, selling stamps over the counter.

After marrying white men, my aunts retired their jobs. They became secret artists, putting up huge amounts of quilts, needlework, and beadwork in the fruit cellars. Sometimes, when husbands and children slept, the aunts slipped into the cellars and gazed at their work. Smoothing an imaginary wrinkle from a quilt, running the embroidery silks through their roughened fingers, threading the beads on a small loom, working the red, blue, and yellow stones. By day, the dutiful wife. By night, sewing and

20

beading their souls into beauty that will be left behind after death, telling the stories of who these women were.

My dad worked in a factory, making cars he never drove. Mama encouraged dad to go to school. Grandma prayed he would go to school. Between the two forces, Daddy decided to make cars in the morning and go to college at night. Mama took care of children for money. Daddy went to school for years. He eventually became a quiet teacher. He loved his work. His ambition, his dream, was to teach on a reservation. There were so many debts from school. We wore hand-me-downs most of our young lives. Daddy had one suit to teach in. When he wore his beaded necklace, some of the students laughed. His retirement came earlier than expected. The white boys in his Indian History class beat him up as they chanted, "Injun Joe, Injun Joe." My mama stopped taking care of children. Now she takes care of Daddy and passes on the family lore to me.

When I was a little girl, Grandpa taught me Mohawk. He thought I was smart. I thought he was magic. He had a special room that was filled with blueprints. When and if he had a job, he'd get out the exotic paper, and I sat very still, watching him work. As he worked, he told me stories. His room smelled of ink, tobacco, and sometimes, forbidden whiskey. Those times were good when I was a little girl. When Grandpa died, I forgot the language. But in my dreams I remember—*raksotha raoka: ra'.**

Margaret had braids that wrapped around her head. It was my delight to unbraid them every night. I would move the brush from the top of her head down through the abundance of silver that was her hair. Once, I brought her hair up to my face. She smelled like smoke and woods. Her eyes were smoke also. Secret fires, banked down. I asked her to tell me about the reserve. She told me her baby had died there, my father's twin. She told me about Eliza. Eliza had dreams of her family flying in the air, becoming seeds

---

*my grandfather's story

21

that sprouted on new ground. The earth is a turtle where new roots bear new fruit. "Eliza gave me life," Grandma said. Grandmother, you have given me my life.

Late at night, pulling the quilt up to cover me, she whispered, "Don't forget who you are. Don't ever leave your family. They are what matters."

For All My Grandmothers

A hairnet covered her head
a net
encasing the silver
a cage
confining the wildness.
No thread escaped.

Once, hair spilling,
you ran through the woods
hair catching on branches
filaments gathered leaves
burrs attached to you.
You sang.
Your bare feet skimmed the earth.

Prematurely taken from the land
giving birth to children
who grew in a world that is white.
Prematurely
you put your hair up
covered it with a net.

Prematurely grey
they called it.

Hairbinding.

Damming the flow.

With no words, quietly
the hair fell out
formed webs on the dresser
on the pillow
in your brush.
These tangled strands
pushed to the back of a drawer
wait for me
to untangle
to comb through
to weave the split fibers
and make a material
strong enough
to encompass our lives.

Robbing Peter to Pay Paul

Her hands moved slowly across the quilting boards. Brown hands with wrinkles, liver spots. Swollen hands, old hands, though the woman can't be much older than sixty.

The top of the quilt has been pieced together by the daughters of the sixty-year-old woman. Now, the final work will be done. The top is stitched to a bottom layer, a bed sheet that Grandma has dyed. Sandwiched in-between—thick layers of cotton batting.

This pattern, *Robbing Peter to Pay Paul*, looks uncomplicated, but a woman's eye can detect the intricacy of the design. Each block is a mirror image of the one beside it, only in a different color and material. So the eyes are dazzled by bright colors next to somber colors, dark colors next to light. Each square has robbed a scrap of cloth from the other.

"Mother, you'll go blind," my aunts would say. Grandma laughed as she pulled her eyeglasses from her face and wiped her tired eyes. "I only have one block to go, just one more. Beth Ellen, do you have those needles threaded yet?" I painstakingly threaded the needles with eight-year-old fingers. The needles were #6 for quilting; the ends were blunted, like Grandma's life.

Grandma belonged to the Turtle Clan. She passed this on to her children, her grandchildren. Her quilts were the shell that covered her, protected us.

Stitch by stitch, block by block. Hands moving across the boards, stealing scraps of cloth to begin a new square. Stealing time for one more block, just one more.

Indian Giver

ONE

Grandpa had chickens. In our backyard in urban Detroit, he had built a coop with little nests, but the chickens ran wild.

He gave them names. Mohawk names. His favorite was Atyo, which means *brother-in-law*. Said that the chicken's eyes had a look in them that reminded him of one of his relatives. It was useless to tell Grandpa that chickens were female and should have female names. He said it didn't matter, now we would have plenty of eggs and poultry to eat. But when it came time to kill the first hen, Grandpa couldn't do it. Said it was like killing one of the family. And didn't Atyo look at him with those eyes, just like brother-in-law, and beg not to have its head chopped off? The hens multiplied.

We had lots of eggs to eat. Grandma and Grandpa even boxed them up and sold them to the neighbors. Grandpa was happy with this arrangement. The rest of us . . . . Well, we had to step lightly in the yard, and Grandma mumbled about hanging clothes on the line and stepping on chicken shit and my, it made a mess of her shoes.

Some of the hens died of natural causes. Some died from Kitty, the twelve-year-old tomcat that bore no resemblance to his name and probably never had. But if we found a dead hen, Grandma and Mama plucked the feathers and made a stew. Pretty tough the meat was, but Grandpa would say, "See this was a good idea of mine; no sense in killing happy chickens. Let them die of their own accord."

We laughed as we chewed and chewed and chewed the tough meat. And ate eggs on the side, of course.

TWO

Each Christmas, Grandma had this plan that we'd have a bigger tree than the year before. The front room was pretty small, but she'd have measured the tree from the previous year, wrote down the measurements in her notebook, and then set out to find the perfect tree for this year. Sometimes it was embarrassing to have Grandma get out her tape measure and measure the trees in the lot down the street. A bunch of us kids had to go with her, each year our number increasing in order to carry the heavy balsam back to our house.

One year we couldn't get the tree through the door. Grandpa came out with a saw.

"Joseph Marcus, what in heaven's name are you going to do?"

"Margaret, there's only one way to get this tree in the house, and that's by cutting off the branches and gluing them back on once we get the tree in the front room."

"You're crazy," Grandma protested. But then, she gave in to the suggestion.

After all the big branches were cut off, we managed to get the tree in the front room where its trunk proved to be too big for the treestand.

Grandma said, "Now what, big smart man?"

He ran to the fruit cellar, coming up with a tin bucket. He got my dad to mix some cement, placed the tree in the bucket, then poured the cement inside. Grandpa said he'd just stand there holding the tree, waiting for the cement to harden. He stood for a long time.

Grandma went into the kitchen to help my mom make the bread for the week. I could hear them in the kitchen, laughing. Grandma and Mom made trips to the front room, Grandma saying, "Still there, smart man?"

"Still here, smart woman."

In the meantime, us kids were collecting sawed-off branches and bringing them in, wondering how Grandpa was going to fix this one. One of us even asked, "Hey Grandpa, how are we going to get these branches back on the tree? It don't seem likely." But Grandpa had faith. He'd find the right branches, they would fit perfectly, and the glue would magically stick.

It didn't work out that way. One thing was that somehow he hadn't held the tree straight, and it leaned to one side. But Grandpa said the leaning side could go towards the window and no one would ever know. Billy, one of the littler kids, said, "Grandpa, it still looks like it's leanin', like it's going to crash through the window."

This time Grandpa didn't answer.

The glue wouldn't stick. Even with all of us holding the branches tight against the trunk, they just fell off.

By now, Grandma was getting mad. But Grandpa retaliated by saying if she didn't have such notions about bigger trees every year, none of this would have happened.

There was truth to this claim, but as Grandma said, "Well, I admit I get notions, but it's too late to talk about that. You, Joseph Marcus, *you* take the cake!"

That Christmas we had this funny tree. But it was even funnier on Christmas morning. Grandma had bought little dolls for all the girls, dolls dressed in their national costumes. It had been her idea to decorate the tree with these dolls perching on branches. Since there were no branches to perch on, Grandpa hated to waste the glue, so he put a drop on each doll's foot and arranged them at intervals around the skinny tree.

On Christmas morning when we came downstairs the dolls looked sort of crazy. Most of them were hanging upside down, skirts over their heads, only their white underpants showing. Trying to get them off the tree was another matter. The kitchen knife was brought forth and each doll sawed off the tree. I had a Spanish doll with a black lace mantilla and a sliver of balsam underneath her feet.

We laughed a lot over that tree, Grandpa saying, "See, I knew it would work out."

The next year, Grandpa nailed the Christmas tree to the floor. But that's another story.

Coyote Learns a New Trick

Coyote thought of a good joke.

She laughed so hard, she almost wanted to keep it to herself. But what good is a joke if you can't trick creatures into believing one thing is true when Coyote knows truth is only what she makes it.

She laughed and snorted and got out her sewing machine and made herself a wonderful outfit. Brown tweed pants with a zipper in the front and very pegged bottoms. A white shirt with pointed collar and french cuffs. A tie from a scrap of brown and black striped silk she had found in her night rummagings. She had some brown cowboy boots in her closet and spit on them, polishing them with her tail. She found some pretty stones that she fashioned into cufflinks for her dress shirt.

She bound her breasts with an old diaper left over from her last litter, and placed over this a sleeveless undershirt that someone had thrown in the garbage dump. It had a few holes and smelled strong, but that went with the trick. She buttoned the white shirt over the holes and smell, and wound the tie around her neck, where she knotted it with flair.

She stuffed more diapers into her underpants so it looked like she had a swell inside. A big swell.

She was almost ready, but needed something to hide her brown hair. Then she remembered a fedora that had been abandoned by an old friend, and set it at an angle over one brown eye.

She looked in the mirror and almost died laughing. She looked like a very dapper male of style.

Out of her bag of tricks, she pulled a long silver chain and looped it from her belt to her pocket, where it swayed so fine.

Stepping outside her lair, she told her pups she'd be back after she had performed this latest bit of magic. They waved her away with, "Oh Mom, what is it this time?"

Subduing her laughter, she walked slowly, wanting each creature to see her movements and behold the wondrous Coyote strutting along.

A hawk spied her, stopped in mid-circle, then flew down to get a good look. "My god, I've never seen anything like it!" And Hawk screamed and carried on, her wing beating her leg as she slapped it with each whoop of laughter. Then she flew back into the sky in hot pursuit of a juicy rat she had seen earlier.

Coyote was undaunted. She knew she looked good, and besides, hawks have been known to have no sense of humor.

Dancing along, Coyote saw Turtle, as usual, caught between the road and the marsh. Stepping more quickly, Coyote approached Turtle and asked, in a sarcastic manner, if Turtle needed directions. Turtle fixed her with an astonished eye and hurriedly moved towards the weeds, grumbling about creatures who were too weird to *even* bother with.

Coyote's plan was not going so well.

Then she thought of Fox. That la-di-da female who was forever grooming her pelt and telling stories about how clever and sly she was. "She's the one!" said Coyote.

So she sauntered up to Fox's place, whistling and perfecting her new deep voice and showful walk. Knocking on Fox's door, she brushed lint and hairs from her shirt, and crushed the hat more securely on her head. Fox opened the door, and her eyes got very large with suprise and admiration.

"Can I help you?" she said with a brush of her eyelashes.

Coyote said, "I seem to be lost. Can you tell a man like me where to find a diner to refresh myself after my long walk?"

Fox said, "Come on in. I was just this minute fixing a little supper and getting ready to have something cool to drink. Won't you join me? It wouldn't do for a stranger to pass through my place and not feel welcomed."

Coyote was impressed. This was going better than she had planned. She stifled a laugh.

"Did you say something?" Fox seemed eager to know.

"I was just admiring your red fur. Mighty pretty."

"Oh, it's nothing. Inherited you know. But I really stand in admiration of your hat and silver chain. Where did you ever find such things?"

"Well, I'm a traveling man myself. Pick up things here and there. Travel mostly at night. You can find a lot of things at night. It sure smells good in here. You must be a fine cook."

Fox laughed, "I've been known to cook up a few things. Food is one of the more sensual pleasures in life, don't you think?" she said, pouring Coyote a glass of red wine. "But I can think of several things that are equally as pleasurable, can't you?" And she winked her red eye. Coyote almost choked on her wine. She realized that she had to get this joke back into her own paws.

"Say, you're a pretty female. Got a man around the house?" Fox laughed and laughed and laughed, her red fur shaking.

"No, there are no men around here. Just me and sometimes a few girlfriends that stay over." And Fox laughed and laughed and laughed, her long nose sniffing and snorting.

33

Coyote couldn't figure out why Fox laughed so much. Maybe she was nervous with such a fine-looking Coyote in her house. Why, I bet she's never seen the likes of me! But it's time to get on with the trick.

Now, Coyote's trick was to make a fool out of Fox. To get her all worked up, thinking Coyote was a male, then reveal her true female Coyote self. It would make a good story. How Fox thought she was so sly and smart, but a Coyote got the best of her. Why, Coyote could tell this story for years to come!

One thing led to another, as they often do. They ate dinner, drank a little more red wine. Fox batted her eyelashes so much, Coyote thought they'd fall off! But Coyote was having a good time too. Now was the time.

"Hey Fox, you seem like a friendly type. How about a roll in the hay?"

"I thought you'd never ask," said Fox, laughing and laughing.

Lying on Fox's pallet, having her body next to hers, Coyote thought maybe she'd wait a bit before playing the trick. Besides, it was fun to be rolling around with a red-haired female. And man oh man, she really could kiss. That tongue of hers sure knows a trick or two. And boy oh boy, that sure feels good, her paw on my back, rubbing and petting. And wow, I never knew foxes could do such things, moving her legs like that, pulling me down on top of her like that. And she makes such pretty noises, moaning like that. And her paw feels real good, unzipping my pants. And oh oh, she's going to find out the trick, and then what'll I do?

"Coyote! Why don't you take that ridiculous stuffing out of your pants. And take off that undershirt, it smells to high heaven. And let me untie that binder so we can get down to *serious* business."

Coyote had not fooled Fox. But somehow, playing the trick didn't seem so important anyway.

So Coyote took off her clothes, laid on top of Fox, her leg moving between Fox's open limbs. She panted and moved and panted some more and told herself that foxes were clever after all. In fact, they were downright smart with all the stuff they knew.

Mmmmm yeah, this Fox is pretty clever with all the stuff she knows. This is the best trick I ever heard of. Why didn't I think of it?

Part Two
DETROIT SONGS

Daddy

"One time I remember," Daddy says.

"The time every day I went out and looked for work. You know, day labor. Everybody standin' in lines, beggin'. We woulda done just about anythin'. Them days, the thirties, we begged!

I heard they was hirin' men at the salt mines, loadin' salt onto the railroad cars. I got there at the right time, cause no sooner had I signed my name on the paper, I was called into the yard. I was lucky that day.

Some men, they was usually white, they got to mine the salt. Go underneath and dig it up. That paid the best. But I was happy with the work. Got hired on for the day. Eight hours. Hard work.

I couldn't talk American. Talked Canadian, eh? They asked me why I talked funny. I says, 'I'm Indian.' So they say, 'Well Chief, get to work.'

Now that mornin' I'd given blood for a friend of mine, laid up in hospital. We had the same type. Indian.

The white woman who took the blood, she said I should relax and take it easy. But those days, you couldn't afford to relax. It was every minute you thought about a job, about feedin' your family. It's the same now. People think about workin', not relaxin'.

Well, I got to workin', throwin' the bags of salt in the box cars. They were heavy. Maybe fifty or a hundred pounds.

We stood in a line, five of us. The line went up, endin' with me on the ladder in front of the box cars. Yes, the salt ended with me. I was the last and threw it in the car. My arms were numb, eh?

Sometimes the bags broke, and the salt came spillin' out on us. The boss yelled and yelled, makin' us sweep it up and put it back in the bags. Some of us, we laughed at him.

I remember, his face was so red, and he worried more about salt than he did about us. But see, that was his job, eh?

That's the way it was in those days. And it's still like that. I never knew anybody a union didn't help.

That day I had a sandwich your ma had made for me. Pork, I think it was. On fry bread. It was in my pocket, wrapped in wax paper, but it made a stain on my pants.

You know how you can remember funny things about the past? Well, that day, I remember the boss's red face and that stain on my pants. And the man I shared my sandwich with.

He was a white man, and he was real hungry. Told me he had a big family, nine or ten kids, I think. Yes, that's what it was.

Well, I ate my part of the sandwich and was gettin' dizzy all the while. I guess the blood-givin' made me a little weak. I don't know if I can make it for the whole eight hours, but I eat some more and sit for a few.

Then the boss asks do I want to work an extra four hours. I say yes! Not thinkin', but still I'm thinkin' about your mom, your sister, your grandma and grandpa. It makes sense to say yes to work.

So I work, eh?

The dizziness went away. I think I scared it.

I got home around eleven o'clock that night. Your mom, she fixes me a bowl of soup and some tea. I go to bed and sleep for twenty-four hours. Straight.

Your mom, she tries to get me up the next day. I can't move. I slept for twenty-four hours!

And the worst part is that I missed goin' out to look for work the next day. Your ma, she was mad, but then she wasn't.

I figure I worked twelve hours in two days and missed out on four more hours work. That made *me* mad.

I never gave blood to an Indian again."

Garnet Lee

"Honey, I was born in Kentucky fifty-six years ago.

Daddy worked in the coal mines. Mommy did cleanin' for the coal mine owners. You could say we was a company family. You could say that.

There was nine of us kids. It were hard on Mommy and Daddy.

When I was a kid, I didn't hold much with learnin'. Mommy was all the time preachin' on us that we needed a education. That it were a one-way ticket outta Grassman's Gulch. Grassman's Gulch, that's where I'm from. The best thing about school was the readin'. We didn't have no libraries, but this lady that were my teacher, well she had millions a books up to her place. She invited some of us up and said we could borrow them. Honey, the books I borrowed woulda filled a house! I was all the time readin'.

I remember this here one about a English lady, name of Jane Eyre. I can remember thinkin', why Garnet Lee, you ain't got it so bad. Leastwise, you got you a mommy and a daddy, and this here little English lady was a orphan. And that were a hundred years ago and things not as easy as they is now. That book stuck in me. Musta read it one hundred times!

In school, like I say, I liked the readin' part. But that other stuff. Lordy, I was thinkin' I must be some kind a dummy!

But I finished my education. On Graduation Day I says to Mommy, 'Well Mommy, where's my one-way ticket outta here?' She and Daddy laughed, fit to kill!

Later on, I was sorry I said what I said after what happened to my daddy. See, Daddy had the black lung. He knew it. Most everybody what worked in the mines had it. But it weren't the black lung got him. It were the explosion.

It seemed like we was always waitin' on that siren to go off. And when it did, you could see the same look passin' over folks' faces—scared to death it were gonna be our daddies or husbands killed.

That's how my daddy died.

When they brought him up from the mine, I thought Mommy was goin' to lose her mind! He were covered in coal dust, and Mommy was a screamin' and a cursin'. 'Wipe that dust offen my man's face, cain't you see he cain't breathe! He gonna die iffen he cain't breathe!'

And she kept on screamin' his name, 'Lewis Joe! Lewis Joe!'

And me bein' the oldest, I couldn't bring my daddy back, and I stood with my arms around my mommy thinkin', Sweet Jesus, how'm I gonna take care of us all? I knowed that were what Mommy was thinkin'. If she could even think beyond that tore-up feeling she had inside.

The women folk, they took the kids for the night. Me and Mommy went back to our place, and some of the ladies stayed with us.

Mommy keened most a the night. In my wildest nightmares I hear that cry that don't sound like nothin' human.

We didn't have no insurance. And the company tried to buy off the relations of the dead men with a compensation. One hundred dollars.

They brought that old envelope up to the house and Mommy opened it and said, 'You mean my man was only worth a hundred dollars? Look again, you thievin' murderers!' And she tore that hundred dollar bill right in little pieces and threw it in Mr. Harvey

Bridgewater's face. I was right proud of Mommy. She looked a fright. Like some haint from down the gulch, her skinny little body just a shakin', and her fists right up to Mr. Bridgewater's nose. That black hair of hers, just a standin' out like a wild woman.

She slammed the door on the company, then says to us kids, 'Listen kids, we goin' to Detroit, Michigan where Aunt May lives. She got her a big heart, and I hope she got even a bigger house, cause we a movin' in!'

Now I was seventeen at the time. With a high school education. Most girls I knew were already married and havin' kids. I was right glad that hadn't happened to me. So I thought, Detroit, here I come, and you better be ready for Garnet Lee Taylor!

I'd been workin' since I was twelve, washin' laundry, cleanin' houses. Even had a little savin's account. Mommy always said I should put some money aside for myself. Said it made a girl proud to have a few dollars to her name. And I was a proud one, sure enough.

We used that money to take the train to Detroit. Lord, that was a trip! Mommy looked real old and tired. She were only thirty-three years old and a old woman afore her time. I swore I was gonna get me a job in one a them factories I heard about and make me some good money. For Mommy and the kids.

We moved to Aunt May's. You know they just welcomed us and made it feel like it were our home too. Mommy looked for work every day. But who was goin' to hire a woman that looked a hundred years old? I only saw Mommy laugh onct or twict while we was livin' at Aunt May's.

But I got a job! Workin' for Chrysler's. I couldn't believe my luck. Them days, they had so many women workin' the factories, because of the war, they didn't want no more. But my cousin Bobby, he was in the union and talked to them high-up people, and they hired me on. It like to kill me! Girl, if there ever was a tired woman, it was me. I'd always worked hard, but this was different.

The noise was so bad. I thought my eardrums would bust. And everything just moved by so fast. I was scared silly. Thought I'd lose my hearin', then my arm.

Them days, there were a big war effort goin' on. I had to learn all kinda things havin' to do with machines. Lordy, I cut myself up some, and not a soul would help me. But I said, 'Garnet Lee Taylor, if you can't do what a bunch a men can do, then you ain't worth your salt.' I was young and healthy. Even had all my teeth then! I made it through, like I knew I would. The men, they called me 'hillbilly,' then wanted to come callin' on me! I said, 'Listen boys, you make a insult with one hand, then hold sugar in the other. Which one *am* I supposed to take?!'

After the war, they wanted to get rid of the ladies right quick. But I stuck to my rights. I belonged to the union by then. My proudest day was when I got my union card. Girl, the U.A.W.!! My daddy died for lack of a union. Garnet Lee Taylor was not goin' to die or be put outta a job. I had a family to raise, just like any man, and they was dependent on me and my job.

I moved Mommy and the kids into a apartment in Hamtramck, not far from the plant. I could walk to work, and we'd save that little extra for the kids' education. Some a the older ones was gettin' restless. You know boys, they wanted to be on their own. But I told them, 'You get you a job and finish that education or you don't come runnin' to me and Mommy for to get you back on your feet!' They was all good kids. Daddy and Mommy did a decent upbringin' on us. The boys got steady jobs. So did the girls. And they weren't no tramps neither! It's funny how when people hear your accent, they think you're trash and treat you like their garbage don't stink same as yours. Some a them northerners was a funny bunch!

I worked side by side a colored man for fifteen years. I learned some by doin' that. Yes, Samuel was a learner to me. Now, work is work, and if you're workin' and doin' what you're supposed to, you ain't got time for that name calling and prejudice stuff. But there were always some didn't like Samuel nor the other colored folk. Just cause their skin was black. Actually, Samuel was a brown man. Brown like the garden dirt, right before spring. Dark and true. I miss that man. He died some years back. Some a his kids workin' at the plant now. I say, if you work with a person long enough, you're just a plain fool if you can't see you're in it together. Workin' people's lives is hard times. You got to stick to each other. It's like bein' in a family. Lord knows, families can be a pain in the you-know-what, but nothin' ain't easy. Yes, workin' people got to stick to each other. Lord knows, the company ain't goin' to!

It seemed like the years just flew away. Pretty soon, there were just Mommy and me. Why, Betty Opal and Louise even went to college. Lewis, Ruth, and Chrystal moved back home. Lew's workin' in the same mine our daddy died in. But Lew's got hisself a union. Ain't nobody goin' to mess with him! I hear they even got women a workin' them mines. Lordy be, my heart goes out to them ladies. I know it must be hard. Wasn't it hard on all us ladies? But you know girl, I always did have a big mouth and a don't-you-mess-in-my-business attitude.

Men. I've had plenty in my life and plenty is more than I needed! But my women friends, now that's another story. I don't have to tell you that when it come to bein' friends, real buddies, ain't nothin' like a woman to help you get over the sorrows of livin'. We have some good times, let me tell you. I'd say that women folk got somethin' special. Tenderness. We can be mean as snakes and then some, but the women, well we got a tender quality too. A right sweetness.

When the plant closed in Hamtramck, I was transferred over here. So me and Mommy bought this here little house in Melvin-dale. We even got us a back yard so's we can grow our flowers and vegetables.

Me, I'm still readin'. Even got me my own copy of Miss Jane Eyre! Mommy says, 'Garnet Lee, we gonna have to move again, to accommodate all these books of yourn.' I just laugh and say, 'Now listen here Mommy, they be wantin' me to retire soon, and we goin' to be two old ladies gettin' in each other's hair. If I don't have my books, I'd just be worryin' you to death. So you go dig in the dirt or watch that twenty-four inch color TV you got. Don't you be teasin' me none about my recreation.'

Mommy come over and kiss me on the cheek and say, 'Honey, you are a right good girl. I be ever so proud a you and your book readin'.'

Tenderness. That's what I'm a talkin' about. You can't say the women ain't got it. You can't never say that."

Terri

"My name is Terri. With an *i*. Yeah, I was born right here in this neighborhood. It don't matter how old I am, let's just say I'm over twenty-one. Ha!

I've been dancing for about two years now. I like it. Five days a week I work at K-Mart as a cashier. It sure gives me something to look forward to, being a go-go-girl on Friday nights. It makes me feel happy to get all dolled up and go out and dance for the ladies. They like me. I think it's my long black hair.

I pick out my outfits real careful. See, I dance three sets, and you gotta have a change of costume for each dance. And I pick my music real careful too. One of my favorites is 'Sweet Dreams.' You know, the Eurythmics. My customers like it. It's kinda sexy and dangerous at the same time. I don't like nothing too disco. Just the sexy stuff.

When I was growing up that's all I had was my looks. But it's something, right? My ma died when I was twelve. She had cancer. Did I tell you my ma was part Indian? Yeah, Chippewa. My dad's a Polack. That's how come I got Indian hair and hazel eyes. Some of the girls here thought I should change my name to Honey on account of the color of my skin. But they thought it should be spelled *Honee*. With two *e*'s. My real name is Theresa Stephanya.

What a name! Ha! A Polack Indian! My black hair comes from my ma. My meanness comes from my dad! But he's okay really. It was hard on him when Ma died. There was five of us kids and dad worked as a custodian for the school. A fancy name for janitor.

I left home when I was seventeen. I had an older girlfriend. Pat. She was some tough butch! Except with me. I'm telling you, what she wouldn't do for me! But still, we broke up when I turned eighteen. I wasn't ready to settle down with one. I wanted them all! Pat comes in here sometimes. She gives me big tips. But she's still jealous after all these years. I remember this fight we had here. Pat and Brenda fighting over me. Pat stuck a pool cue in Brenda's stomach. It was a mess. Brenda got sewed up and she was back the next week, laying fives and tens on me. Ha!

I don't get paid any money for dancing. We all just do it for tips and for . . . I don't know, maybe being some kind of star. Pat says I have show biz blood in me. I love the clapping and the whistles and the music and the spinning around in my fancy clothes. I like the tips, too! And these girls don't want nothing from you. They just like to watch and appreciate you. I worked a straight bar once and hated it. The men thought you were a whore and put their hands on you till you wanted to puke. *And* they were lousy tippers. But the girls here, they don't want nothing. Oh, maybe they got a little thought that they'd like to take you home and set up a place and you could be their old lady. But who cares, right? Every butch wants a pretty lady at home and someone to show off. And every girl like me wants somebody to take care of them and love them. It all suits me fine.

I love pretty clothes. All my girlfriends buy me clothes. I must have about twenty sweaters in different colors. When I was thirteen, I told my dad all I wanted for Christmas was a red sweater made from real angora. But I knew I wouldn't get it. Who had the

50

money? When my ma was alive she used to make Christmas so fun! We had a tree and Ma made decorations and one time she bought a real glass star for the top. I took that star with me when I moved out. I promised myself that when I got my own place I'd always have a tree and make it a real Christmas. And I have. And that glass star looks prettier every year.

But I do love clothes. And my favorite color is red. You probably guessed that. Ha! My favorite dancing outfit is a bright red teddy trimmed in black lace. I wear my red satin heels and my black stockings with the rhinestones up the sides. And I always wear a flower in my hair. I've sort of got this bit where the flower falls out, and I pick it up and throw it to the girls sitting out there. They love it.

This place is sort of home to me. Friday nights I dance, and then we go out and party after the bar closes. Saturday nights I come here and drink and talk with my pals. We're pretty close all of us. The time Wanda's girlfriend died and she wasn't allowed at the funeral, we had a big wake here. Everybody brought food, and we played all their favorite songs, and we cried a little. We love Wanda. She's one of us. This is a family.

When I was little, Ma made us a family. But when she died, we sort of broke up. Ma told the best stories. I think I get my dramatic flair from her. She grew up in Detroit, but her dad was raised on a reservation, and she sort of handed down his stories to me. I don't got any kids, but when I dance I feel like that's kinda like telling a story. You know what I mean? I want the ladies who paid good money to see me to get in a mood that makes them happy. It's not just wanting to do a good job for the tips, but I want to do a good job for them. And the outfits and the music and the dancing, it's all sort of . . . I don't know, like a present or something. Like I can give everybody a present. Maybe it sounds crazy, but that's the way I am. Do you know what I'm saying?"

Mama

"There was a time when I was watching seven kids at a time," Mama says. "I never thought about getting tired. From 6:30 to 6:00, all those kids. My lord, I must have been desperate!

Let's see, there was Sarah and Claudine, Gerry, Alice and Bobby, Alan and Benita. Plus the two of you. My stars, all those kids! Such a cramped-up house.

But you know it was extra money. It made a difference, no doubt about it. And no taxes to pay either.

Your dad, he laughed at me and those kids. Said, 'Hazel, you sure like kids, don't you?' To tell the truth, I did like kids. Still do. But that was too many. I never knew how the girl across the street did it. You remember Cookie? Twelve kids! Catholics. I always said if those priests had to take care of children, you can bet there wouldn't be no rules about birth control!

One time, Bobby got worms. I was deathly afraid that the rest of the children would get them, and then the mothers would take away my job. If you get a reputation for a dirty house, well you can forget about babysitting for a job.

I scrubbed the whole house down with Lysol and alcohol. That's what I heard was good to get rid of the eggs. Don't ask me how he

53

picked them up. I suspect it was from school. But I killed them off, those eggs. I boiled the sheets and towels and all the clothes.

Your grandma was a great help to me, and so was your grandpa while he was still alive. He never thought it was beneath him to watch children and clean house. How's that for women's lib?

At night I'd be so tired, your dad and me didn't have a chance to visit. You girls felt slighted I know. But that's the way it was. I never thought about doing different.

I'd only gone through high school. Didn't have much of a skill. Oh, I could type, but nothing fancy. The jobs I had were working at Woolworth's and at the grocery shop. I remember I had to turn over all my wages to my father back then. I think I was making twenty-five cents a week! Then when I married your dad, I took in ironing and did some laundry work.

Once, I worked in a doctor's office. I learned a lot there. I learned to give shots, which came in real handy after your grandma got diabetes. And when you came down with rheumatic fever, we saved a lot of money by me giving you your penicillin.

Watching those kids wasn't easy. But they were sweet. I never had a bad one. And the older ones helped out. You and your sister helped too.

I suppose, when I think about it, I didn't get paid very much to watch other people's children. It's always been that way. People don't think baby-sitting is a worthwhile job.

I once thought that when I stopped watching kids, maybe I'd see if the hospitals could use a woman to sit and rock the babies in the nursery, or change diapers, some such work as that. But they were only hiring on nurses' aides and told me that aides don't get to hold babies or have anything to do with them. Seemed as though you had to have a degree to know how to hold babies. Imagine that! I was kind of disappointed. Then I got pregnant with your baby brother and figured I'd have my own baby to rock.

But I watched kids up until your brother was born. Then after, I started up again. It seemed there were always bills that needed the extra money. And you girls were getting big and wanting nice things. Even though we couldn't afford them most of the time, you weren't so bad off, were you?

One time, I saved off a dollar a week. Put it away. Didn't tell anyone, not even your dad. Then that Christmas I bought you and your sister Garland sweaters. Remember those? You girls were so thrilled.

I was never ashamed of what I did. It was decent work, taking care of children. I was never ashamed of what I did."

Danny

"My dad worked for Ford's. What else do people do around here? Ma worked as a waitress. Man, she'd come home so fucked over and tired, I used to want to kill! Guys all the time putting the make on her. Ma was real pretty, and Dad was jealous. I could hear them fight when I was a kid. Me and Sean and Joey would hear him yelling at her, saying she was coming on to the men in the diner. But she wasn't. She was just real pretty. It seems like when you're a kid, you gotta take sides sometimes. I always took Ma's side.

I was a pretty kid. Wanted to be like my ma. Wanted to be a girl. Sean teased me a lot, called me 'sissy.' But Joey stood up for me. Man, I loved Joey so much. He was everything a kid should be. He was strong and good in sports. But he had this sweet side to him. He used to cry when Dad got on my case about something. And that was a lot.

In a way, I couldn't blame Dad. Christ, he worked like a dog for Mr. Henry Ford so Mr. Henry Ford could live in Grosse Pointe, and have fancy houses all over the world, and be a big man. Dad thought he wasn't a man. That's why he pushed us around. Made him feel like somebody. Shit man, here we were, living in a crummy house in Lincoln Park, trying to take care of our lives. And some people on the street still talking like it was a century ago—calling us 'dirty Irish,' 'shanty pigs.' Man, I just couldn't relate to any of it. There was always so much ugliness, you know?

Early on, I liked to dress in Ma's clothes. I guess I knew it was something I shouldn't be doing, but I wanted to be pretty and dressing up made me feel pretty. I got caught once. Dad gave me a big talk about being a man. Then he beat the shit outta me to prove his point. Ma, well she asked me why I was doing it. I couldn't answer her because I didn't know.

By the time I got to high school, I was a real hippie. Wore my hair long and in a braid. God, the shit really flew! Dad threatening to throw me out of the house, calling me a 'bum.' Joey trying to make peace all the time. Ma asking me if I wanted to see a psychiatrist. Man, she could hardly spell it, let alone know what they were for! Ma, she tried so hard with me.

Me, I talked trash to my folks and told them all to fuck off.

I took a lot of drugs. Man, there wasn't anything I wouldn't try. Christ, I couldn't make it in school if I wasn't stoned all the time.

I liked guys. Used to dream about them. It never failed, I always went for the butch types. You know, football players, jock types. But they were too busy proving what men they were—fucking girls, then bragging about it.

I moved out when I was sixteen. Moved in with Joey, who was nineteen and working in a garage. I had a job after school cutting up vegetables for this Italian restaurant. I got to eat whatever I wanted, and the old lady who owned the place really liked me. She used to tell me I was a good boy. Jesus, if she only knew what a pervert I was.

Somehow, I kept in school till I graduated. Then I thought that what I really wanted to do was to be a nurse. Working-class dreams!

I enrolled in this program. Got some loans. Joey and Ma gave me some money. The old man thought I had really gone off the deep end with this one. But hell, it was a job and a job that paid off in some ways. Or at least that's what I thought.

I was the only man in the program. But it was okay. I always liked being with women, but I knew they'd think I was a freak if they ever saw me in the dress I used to wear at night.

Finally, I became a nurse. Got my job at Children's Hospital working in the Emergency Room. Nothing prepared me for what I saw in the E.R. Little kids all beat up from their fucker fathers. Little girls bleeding and dying from some bastard's prick.

God, I hated being a man, if that's what men were!

I met my first boyfriend at the hospital. He worked in x-ray. A real sweet guy. Reminded me of Joey. We wanted to live together, but it didn't work out. He didn't like that I wanted to dress like a woman sometimes. Said it made him feel funny. I could dig it, but it's like I *had* to do it, you know?

I sort of decided that I'd just do my thing and do my work, and life would just go along. So that's what I did.

On my nights off, I'd dress up and go down to the Corridor and parade myself. And it really was a parade. Freaks on display. Danny, the biggest freak of all. You know, there were some real sickos down there. Straight-looking guys in business suits picking up queers like me. They weren't honest, you know?

I could see myself as an old man doing this, and it scared the shit out of me. That's when I started thinking I wouldn't live to be thirty. I couldn't see any other kind of life for me.

I worked hard at the hospital. See, I liked the kids. Wanted to take the hurt away. Sometimes, I'd see the same kids over and over. We'd patch them up and the hospital would let them go back to their fucked-up lives.

Man, I wanted to blow up the world! And all the goddamn fucking bastards with it!

I used to take Valium after work to calm myself down. I stole an IV and gave it to myself that way. I'd watch it drip into my veins and think each drop was some kid's life. Crazy, huh?

The last night of my life, I got this idea to dress up in my red dress and go to the Interchange. What the fuck! It was my life, right?

At the funeral parlor, they cut my hair off, but that night it was still long. I didn't need to wear wigs like some of the boys. I was wearing those turquoise earrings you gave me. I hope you got them back. One crazy night I wrote down everything I wanted my friends to have. Joey got my guitar.

Maybe I did know something would happen to me. Man, I was so full of junk and shit, I couldn't tell whether or not I was dead or alive anyway.

I went to the Interchange. Picked up a queer. We were leaving the bar when these two dudes stopped us. The one says, 'Hey, we're the vice squad, let me see your wallet.' Shit, now I knew these dudes weren't the cops, just some kids hassling queers.

So I says, like the asshole I am, 'Get lost fucker. If you want my money, you'll have to kill me.'

The last thing I remember was him pulling out a gun and aiming it at my crotch. Then he shot me. Blew me away. For good measure, he put a bullet in my head. Wanted to make sure the freak was put away.

So, there's one less queer on the streets, and I guess that means that respectable people are resting easier in their lives. Or, most likely, they don't even know I'm gone."

Her Name Is Helen

Her name is Helen.
She came from Washington State twenty years ago through
broken routes
of Hollywood, California,
Gallup, New Mexico,
Las Vegas, Nevada,
ended up in Detroit, Michigan where she lives in #413
in the gut of the city.
She worked in a factory for ten years, six months, making
carburetors for Cadillacs.
She loved factory work.
She made good money, took vacations to New Orleans.
"A real party town."

She wears a cowboy hat with pretty feathers.
Can't wear cowboy boots because of the arthritis
that twists her feet.
She wears beige vinyl wedgies. In the winter she pulls on
heavy socks to protect her bent toes from the slush and rain.

Helen takes pictures of herself.

Everytime she passes those Polaroid booths,
one picture for a dollar,
she closes the curtain and the camera flashes.

When she was laid off from the factory
she got a job in a bar, serving up shots and beer.
Instead of tips, she gets presents from her customers.
Little wooden statues of Indians in headdress.
Naked pictures of squaws with braided hair.
Feather roach clips in fuschia and chartreuse.
Everybody loves Helen.
She's such a good guy. An honest-to-god Indian.

Helen doesn't kiss.
She allows her body to be held when she's had enough
vodkas and Lite beer.
She's had lots of girlfriends.
White women who wanted to take care of her,
who liked Indians,
who think she's a tragedy.

Helen takes pictures of herself.

She has a picture on a keychain, along with a baby's shoe
and a feathered roach clip.
She wears her keys on a leather belt.
Helen sounds like a chime, moving behind the bar.

Her girlfriends took care of her.
Told her what to wear
what to say
how to act more like an Indian.
"You should be proud of your Indian heritage.
Wear more jewelry.
Go to the Indian Center."

Helen doesn't talk much.
Except when she's had enough
vodkas and Lite beer.
Then she talks about home,
about her mom,
about the boarding schools,
the foster homes,
about wanting to go back to see her people
before she dies.
Helen says she's going to die when she's fifty.

She's forty-two now.
Eight years to go.

Helen doesn't kiss.
Doesn't talk much.
Takes pictures of herself.

She touches women who are white.
She is touched by their hands.

Helen can't imagine that she is beautiful.
That her skin is warm
like redwood and fire.
That her thick black hair moves like a current.
That her large body speaks in languages stolen from her.
That her mouth is wide and full and when she smiles
people catch their breath.

"I'm a gay Indian girl.
A dumb Indian.
A fat, ugly squaw."
This is what Helen says.

She wears a t-shirt with the legend
Detroit
splashed in glitter across her large breasts.
Her breasts that white women have sucked
and molded to fit their mouths.

Helen can't imagine that there are women
who see her.
That there are women
who want to taste her breath and salt.
Who want a speech to be created between their tongues.
Who want to go deep inside her
touch places that are dark, wet,
muscle and spirit.
Who want to swell, expand two bodies into a word
of our own making.

Helen can't imagine that she is beautiful.

She doesn't kiss.
Doesn't talk much.
Takes pictures of herself so she will know she is there.

Takes pictures of herself to prove she is alive.

Helen takes pictures of herself.

Part Three
LONG STORIES

The Fifth Floor, 1967

for Mary Moran

The mental ward is on the fifth floor of the county hospital. Inmates joke that it is put there to make escape difficult. As soon as I arrive I am given Thorazine in a tiny pleated paper cup. Orange juice is supposed to mask the taste, but the sharp chemical burn breaks through. I make my first mistake by asking what it is that I am swallowing. Pencil eyebrows rising into brown bangs, the nurse tells me it will calm me down. But I am already calm. I walked here myself, my husband holding my arm.

Why I am here has something to do with losing myself. I used to be there—a young wife and mother in my house—washing dishes, bleaching diapers, reading a book, watching TV. Then I lost me. My husband tells me I am not myself. He tells the nurse and she scrutinizes me, then takes me to a room which is to be mine for the duration. I am to share it with another woman who is not there.

This room has a window. The window has bars growing from the cement sill. When I look out, I see the roof of the other part of the hospital. It is summer, and the roof is wet from the air conditioning units used in administration and operating rooms. The nurse sweats from the heat. I do not sweat. Inside me there is salt. Drying up fluid.

69

I begin to get out my cigarettes and am told that I may carry cigarettes with me but only nurses and orderlies are allowed to carry matches and lighters. I realize I will have to chain smoke. To light one cigarette from another. To avoid asking for anything. I am told that I am free to move from my room to the game room. The game room has TV, Monopoly, and Clue. But no books. It is something to do with too much stimulation. And if we wish to write letters, paper and pen will be supplied by nurse and our writing activity will be supervised. I am a piece of cloth—useless, with no pattern. "Say goodbye to your husband." I say goodbye to this man I thought I recognized but no longer do. He brought me here and signed a white piece of paper. After that I belonged to them, not him. But I am free to roam the halls. Until night.

In one week I have adjusted well. Each morning at 6:00 A.M. we are wakened. I am allowed to take a shower. I am allowed to wash my hair once a week. I keep it braided and it hangs on my back, oily, each strand separated by comb marks. My head looks like a wet clay pot, designs ringed around the outside.

We get to wear our own clothes. This is a new age in the caretaking of crazy people. "The wearing of their own clothes will give a sense of being in familiar surroundings." For this trip I have brought cotton shorts and blouses. A mini-dress of blue plaid. Sneakers and flats. Knee socks, no nylons. My summer nightgown. Underwear from Sears in white cotton.

In one week I haven't eaten. This seems to disturb the nurses who have to write it down on their charts. At first they cajole me with milk. The perfect food. Then they tell me that Doctor says I will have to be force-fed or fed intravenously. Then they say I will have to begin shock treatments if I don't eat. I have seen the patients who come from shock. Their faces are smooth and shiny. It's as if the electric wires have brushed over their skin, leaving an area like a healed burn—flat, glossy. Their eyes don't focus. I even saw a woman's eyes turn from brown to blue. Their bodies jerk. They have to be reminded over and over and over who they are. And where they are. One of the orderlies brings me a Coke from the machine. I take a drink, and there is relief and triumph in the nurse's face. "That's a good girl."

It looks like I will be here for a while. My husband comes twice a week. I don't wish to see him, but I must find out how my children are. He says they are staying at my mother's. He sees them some nights after work. I never think to ask why he can't take them home so they can sleep in their own beds. It is assumed he is helpless. He has enough on his mind with me.

Next week, if I'm good, I will be allowed phone privileges once a day. I will be allowed to go to occupational therapy. I will be allowed to help the other women clean the game room. I drink my Thorazine-laced orange juice twice a day. If I'm good, it will be cut to once a day. Thorazine is not addictive. It turns the brain into cheesecloth. It causes cancer. Nothing sticks to a cheesecloth brain. My eyes are veiled in dotted swiss.

I have not spoken with the other patients who walk the halls with me. I feel the salt inside my body moving through my veins. I am surprised I am not dead. Dried like a fish, salted and ready to eat. I sit in the game room. Watching TV.

At night I look for myself. Between each bed check and the flashlight in my face, I feel my body, seeking a relationship with myself. I wish to know this woman. During the day I pass the mirror hung high on the wall. I try to look for me but see instead a skinny woman with eyes that have no lids. Her hair will not stay tied. It falls out of the ribbon and moves down her back like a ripple or a tidal wave.

71

At home this woman was a crybaby, but the tears never came out of her eyes. They spilled inside her skin, soaking her brain, trickling down the shelves of bones, coming out of her cunt and hands. She left trails of wet salt on her chair, in her bed.

She would not allow her husband to fuck her. She told him his penis would shrivel and die from the wet salt. But he never listened. He climbed on her, shoving his cock against her face, coming in her mouth. She wiped the semen away, rinsing her head under the bathroom faucet.

She dared not touch her daughters or their skin would stain. Their beautiful faces would scar from the wet salt. She sat in her rocker, listening to her daughters' chatter, telling them not to climb on her lap. She would hurt them with hot salt.

Her mother came to see what was wrong. She has heard from the son-in-law that something is wrong. Her mother sees a clean house —everything washed and starched. The children look afraid. The baby has dirty diapers, the middle one is wringing her hands, the eldest is heating a bottle for the youngest. Her mother asks the young wife what is the matter. She answers, "Inside me there are holes where the salt has eaten through. I am turning into the Great Salt Lake. Or a glacier. White and cold."

The mother calls the father. As he comes through the doorway, he instinctively holds up his hands to his face. Warding off a spirit. He says, "We must take her home, bring the babies, heal her." His face tears over. This is his favorite daughter. The one who understands his Indian ways, his talk, his dreams, his lapses into alcohol. She is the one who knows who she is.

They take her home. She is a piece of cloth, ready to be folded in fours, tucked away in a drawer. She was brought here. There are experts who know about such things.

I explore the body of this woman. Hastily. Her breasts are flaccid and numb. I pinch her nipples, feel them rise. I place my hands at her waist, feel her ribs. Her rib cage is wide and round, like staves of a basket. Her thighs are cold and thin. I stroke the soft place of her inner thighs with both hands. Her skin becomes warmer. She trembles with each brush of my fingers. The hair of her cunt is straight and heavy and thick. I touch the slit, the opening of her cunt, the inside of her. She is wet and open. Her clitoris pulses under my finger. I touch her there. Try to find her. She is wet and open. I taste her juice off my finger. She is tart, like sweat and medicine. Both hands attempt to enter her, to go up inside her hole, to touch a place in her that will tell me who I am. I rub her clit. She spasms and comes on my hand, the syrup from her coating my fingers. I bring my hand to my mouth and suck myself to sleep. I have dreams about her. She looks in the mirror, and I see with her eyes.

In occupational therapy I am told I have a choice of making a trivet or an ashtray. The therapist is young and white. Her face is filled with school optimism. She will do her best, and maybe she will get through to some of us. What she doesn't know is that others have already gone through us. We drip water, blood, and salt on the clean white floor. We are uncooperative and strange. But she knows how to handle us: she talks in a perky, determined manner and ignores the strangeness.

The O.T. room is a large room with cupboards lining the walls. Everything seems to be formica. The speckled surfaces gleam from polish. There are boxes of material here and there on the floor. Scraps of cloth, chenille pipe cleaners, plastic reeds for weaving baskets, hanks of acrylic for the loom. But the loom is silent. We are not taught to use it. It has something to do with our brains not being able to comprehend the instruction.

Next to the loom is a kitchenette. We wonder at its use. There are never any signs of anyone having been there. Never an apron hung by the sink, a teakettle resting on a burner. We assume it is put there to remind us of what is normal and therefore unattainable to us. Some of the patients have been here before.

I sit quietly, waiting my turn. "Do you want to make an ashtray or a trivet?" I am overwhelmed by choice. And I watch the others create their escape routes out of the fifth floor. I grab the box of plastic tiles. Begin to sort through the colors. I pick out blue and green. I will make a trivet. Hang it on the kitchen wall at home. The sun will strike the tiles at a certain time of day. For a moment the kitchen will look like how I imagine the ocean to be. The colors will amuse my daughters. The baby will laugh and reach out her hand to touch color. I will make a trivet.

At night I look for myself. Beneath the covers, underneath the bed. In the extra drawer. I touch her body, anxious for the darkness to cover my hands. The flashlights in my face have ceased to bother me. I pretend to be asleep, to have my hands primly on top of the sheets. The woman waits underneath to feel my delicate fingers probing her holes. She opens herself to me. There is no sound between us. Except once, a sigh. She is always open. Open and wet. She is wet and opening up to me. My fingers go deeper. I have touched her insides. Her insides are soft and uncovered and give up secrets. Her breasts are no longer passive. Her thighs are not cool. She is open to me. Inside there is a magic place of wetness. A fiery house. I touch her. She opens.

I will be released in one week. I have begun to eat mashed potatoes, red meat, white bread, and to drink lots of black coffee. The Thorazine has been cut completely. They give me something else, in a capsule. I have behaved well. I pretend to smile at the nurses and orderlies.

74

I have not found me—yet—but the psychiatrist looked at my chart and my good behavior. Besides, my insurance will not pay beyond six weeks of treatment. And I do not have the resources to stay longer. Six weeks. Six weeks to make a crazy woman sane.

I am taking the woman with me. I am smuggling her out. She will go with me as my secret. During these six weeks her face has begun to take on my features. My face has begun to take on lines, and my skin is toughening. Her hair has one thread of silver. My hair is getting darker and thinner. Her body is round, and when my fingers press her thighs, white marks appear which quickly fill with blood, leaving her skin soft, brown, and beautiful. My breasts feel everything. In my dreams, I remember my first-born suckling from me. I awake to wet spots on my nightgown. Inside me there is salt. At times it seeps from my eyes, dropping on my hands. Her body is not salted. Inside her is blood, muscle, electric pulses, and rage. Her fingers send currents through mine. Her fingers are long and rough and there are cracks in her nails. My hands are also rough, and my palms are lined.

I am taking the woman home with me. It is our secret. She keeps me alive.

A Long Story

Dedicated to my Great-Grandmothers
Eliza Powless and Catherine Brant

"About 40 Indian children took the train at this depot for the Philadelphia Indian School last Friday. They were accompanied by the government agent, and seemed a bright looking lot."

The Northern Observer
(Massena, New York, July 20, 1892)

"I am only beginning to understand what it means for a mother to lose a child."

Anna Demeter, *Legal Kidnapping*
(Beacon Press, Boston, 1977)

1890

It has been two days since they came and took the children away. My body is greatly chilled. All our blankets have been used to bring me warmth. The women keep the fire blazing. The men sit. They talk among themselves. We are frightened by this sudden child-stealing. We signed papers, the agent said. This gave them rights to take our babies. It is good for them, the agent said. It will make them civilized, the agent said. I do not know *civilized*.

I hold myself tight in fear of flying apart in the air. The others try to feed me. Can they feed a dead woman? I have stopped talking. When my mouth opens, only air escapes. I have used up my sound screaming their names—She Sees Deer! He Catches The Leaves! My eyes stare at the room, the walls of scrubbed wood, the floor of dirt. I know there are people here, but I cannot see them. I see a darkness, like the lake at New Moon. Black, unmoving. In the center, a picture of my son and daughter being lifted onto the train. My daughter wearing the dark blue, heavy dress. All of the girls dressed alike. Never have I seen such eyes! They burn into my head even now. My son. His hair cut. Dressed as the white men, his arms and legs covered by cloth that made him sweat. His face, streaked with tears. So many children crying, screaming. The sun on our bodies, our heads. The train screeching like a crow, sounding like laughter. Smoke and dirt pumping out of the insides of the train. So many people. So many children. The women, standing as if in prayer, our hands lifted, reaching. The dust sifting down on our palms. Our palms making motions at the sky. Our fingers closing like the claws of the bear.

I see this now. The hair of my son held in my hands. I rub the strands, the heavy braids coming alive as the fire flares and casts a bright light on the black hair. They slip from my fingers and lie coiled on the ground. I see this. My husband picks up the braids, wraps them in cloth; he takes the pieces of our son away. He walks outside, the eyes of the people on him. I see this. He will find a bottle and drink with the men. Some of the women will join him. They will end the night by singing or crying. It is all the same. I see this. No sounds of children playing games and laughing. Even the dogs have ceased their noise. They lay outside each doorway, waiting. I hear this. The voices of children. They cry. They pray. They call me. *Nisten ha.* I hear this. *Nisten ha.* *

1978

I am wakened by the dream. In the dream my daughter is dead. Her father is returning her body to me in pieces. He keeps her heart. I thought I screamed . . . *Patricia!* I sit up in bed, swallowing

---

* mother

78

air as if for nourishment. The dream remains in the air. I rise to go to her room. Ellen tries to lead me back to bed, but I have to see once again. I open her door. She is gone. The room empty, lonely. They said it was in her best interests. How can that be? She is only six, a baby who needs her mothers. She loves us. This has not happened. I will not believe this. Oh god, I think I have died.

Night after night, Ellen holds me as I shake. Our sobs stifling the air in our room. We lie in our bed and try to give comfort. My mind can't think beyond last week when she left. I would have killed him if I'd had the chance! He took her hand and pulled her to the car. The look in his eyes of triumph. It was a contest to him, Patricia the prize. He will teach her to hate us. He will! I see her dear face. That face looking out the back window of his car. Her mouth forming the words *Mommy, Mama.* Her dark braids tied with red yarn. Her front teeth missing. Her overalls with the yellow flower on the pocket, embroidered by Ellen's hands. So lovingly she sewed the yellow wool. Patricia waiting quietly until she was finished. Ellen promising to teach her designs — chain stitch, french knot, split stitch. How Patricia told everyone that Ellen made the flower just for her. So proud of her overalls.

I open the closet door. Almost everything is gone. A few things hang there limp, abandoned. I pull a blue dress from the hanger and take it back to my room. Ellen tries to take it from me, but I hold on, the soft blue cotton smelling of my daughter. How is it possible to feel such pain and live? "Ellen?!" She croons my name. "Mary, Mary, I love you." She sings me to sleep.

1890

The agent was here to deliver a letter. I screamed at him and sent curses his way. I threw dirt in his face as he mounted his horse. He thinks I'm a crazy woman and warns me, "You better settle down

79

Annie." What can they do to me? I am a crazy woman. This letter hurts my hand. It is written in their hateful language. It is evil, but there is a message for me.

I start the walk up the road to my brother. He works for the whites and understands their meanings. I think about my brother as I pull the shawl closer to my body. It is cold now. Soon there will be snow. The corn has been dried and hangs from our cabin, waiting to be used. The corn never changes. My brother is changed. He says that *I* have changed and bring shame to our clan. He says I should accept the fate. But I do not believe in the fate of child-stealing. There is evil here. There is much wrong in our village. My brother says I am a crazy woman because I howl at the sky every evening. He is a fool. I am calling the children. He says the people are becoming afraid of me because I talk to the air and laugh like the raven overhead. But I am talking to the children. They need to hear the sound of me. I laugh to cheer them. They cry for us.

This letter burns my hands. I hurry to my brother. He has taken the sign of the wolf from over the doorway. He pretends to be like those who hate us. He gets more and more like the child-stealers. His eyes move away from mine. He takes the letter from me and begins the reading of it. I am confused. This letter is from two strangers with the names Martha and Daniel. They say they are learning civilized ways. Daniel works in the fields, growing food for the school. Martha cooks and is being taught to sew aprons. She will be going to live with the schoolmaster's wife. She will be a live-in girl. What is a *live-in girl?* I shake my head. The words sound the same to me. I am afraid of Martha and Daniel, these strangers who know my name. My hands and arms are becoming numb.

I tear the letter from my brother's fingers. He stares at me, his eyes traitors in his face. He calls after me, "Annie! Annie!" That is not my name! I run to the road. That is not my name! There is no Martha! There is no Daniel! This is witch work. The paper burns and burns. At my cabin, I quickly dig a hole in the field. The earth

80

is hard and cold, but I dig with my nails. I dig, my hands feeling weaker. I tear the paper and bury the scraps. As the earth drifts and settles, the names Martha and Daniel are covered. I look to the sky and find nothing but endless blue. My eyes are blinded by the color. I begin the howling.

1978

When I get home from work, there is a letter from Patricia. I make coffee and wait for Ellen, pacing the rooms of our apartment. My back is sore from the line, bending over and down, screwing the handles on the doors of the flashy cars moving by. My work protects me from questions, the guys making jokes at my expense. But some of them touch my shoulder lightly and briefly as a sign of understanding. The few women, eyes averted or smiling in sympathy. No one talks. There is no time to talk. No room to talk, the noise taking up all space and breath.

I carry the letter with me as I move from room to room. Finally I sit at the kitchen table, turning the paper around in my hands. Patricia's printing is large and uneven. The stamp has been glued on halfheartedly and is coming loose. Each time a letter arrives, I dread it, even as I long to hear from my child. I hear Ellen's key in the door. She walks into the kitchen, bringing the smell of the hospital with her. She comes toward me, her face set in new lines, her uniform crumpled and stained, her brown hair pulled back in an imitation of a french twist. She knows there is a letter. I kiss her and bring mugs of coffee to the table. We look at each other. She reaches for my hand, bringing it to her lips. Her hazel eyes are steady in her round face.

I open the letter. *Dear Mommy. I am fine. Daddy got me a new bike. My big teeth are coming in. We are going to see Grandma for my birthday. Daddy got me new shoes. Love, Patricia.* She doesn't ask about Ellen. I imagine her father standing over her, coaxing her, coaching her. The letter becomes ugly. I tear it in bits and scatter them out the window. The wind scoops the pieces into a tight fist before strewing them in the street. A car drives over the paper, shredding it to garbage and mud.

Ellen makes a garbled sound. "I'll leave. If it will make it better, I'll leave." I quickly hold her as the dusk moves into the room and covers us. "Don't leave. Don't leave." I feel her sturdy back shiver against my hands. She kisses my throat, and her arms tighten as we move closer. "Ah Mary, I love you so much." As the tears threaten our eyes, the taste of salt is on our lips and tongues. We stare into ourselves, touching the place of pain, reaching past the fear, the guilt, the anger, the loneliness.

We go to our room. It is beautiful again. I am seeing it new. The sun is barely there. The colors of cream, brown, green mixing with the wood floor. The rug with its design of wild birds. The black ash basket glowing on the dresser, holding a bouquet of dried flowers bought at a vendor's stand. I remember the old woman, laughing and speaking rapidly in Polish as she wrapped the blossoms in newspaper. Ellen undresses me as I cry. My desire for her breaking through the heartbreak we share. She pulls the covers back, smoothing the white sheets, her hands repeating the gestures done at work. She guides me onto the cool material. I watch her remove the uniform of work. An aide to nurses. A healer of spirit.

She comes to me full in flesh. My hands are taken with the curves and soft roundness of her. She covers me with the beating of her heart. The rhythm steadies me. Heat is centering me. I am grounded by the peace between us. I smile at her face above me, round like a moon, her long hair loose and touching my breasts. I take her breast in my hand, bring it to my mouth, suck her as a woman—in desire, in faith. Our bodies join. Our hair braids together on the pillow. Brown, black, silver, catching the last light of the sun. We kiss, touch, move to our place of power. Her mouth, moving over my body, stopping at curves and swells of skin, kissing, removing pain. Closer, close, together, woven, my legs are heat, the center of my soul is speaking to her, I am sliding into her, her mouth is medicine, her heart is the earth, we are dancing with flying arms, I shout, I sing, I weep salty liquid, sweet and warm it coats her throat. This is my life. I love you Ellen, I love you Mary, I love, we love.

1891

The moon is full. The air is cold. This cold strikes at my flesh as I remove my clothes and set them on fire in the withered corn field. I cut my hair, the knife sawing through the heavy mass. I bring the sharp blade to my arms, legs, and breasts. The blood trickles like small red rivers down my body. I feel nothing. I throw the tangled webs of my hair into the flames. The smell, like a burning animal, fills my nostrils. As the fire stretches to touch the stars, the people come out to watch me—the crazy woman. The ice in the air touches me.

They caught me as I tried to board the train and search for my babies. The white men tell my husband to watch me. I am dangerous. I laugh and laugh. My husband is good only for tipping bottles and swallowing anger. He looks at me, opening his mouth and making no sound. His eyes are dead. He wanders from the cabin and looks out on the corn. He whispers our names. He calls after the children. He is a dead man.

Where have they taken the children? I ask the question of each one who travels the road past our door. The women come and we talk. We ask and ask. They say there is nothing we can do. The white man is like a ghost. He slips in and out where we cannot see. Even in our dreams he comes to take away our questions. He works magic that resists our medicine. This magic has made us

83

weak. What is the secret about them? Why do they want our children? They sent the Blackrobes many years ago to teach us new magic. It was evil! They lied and tricked us. They spoke of gods who would forgive us if we believed as they do. They brought the rum with the cross. This god is ugly! He killed our masks. He killed our men. He sends the women screaming at the moon in terror. They want our power. They take our children to remove the inside of them. Our power. They steal our food, our sacred rattle, the stories, our names. What is left?

I am a crazy woman. I look to the fire that consumes my hair and see their faces. My daughter. My son. They still cry for me, though the sound grows fainter. The wind picks up their keening and brings it to me. The sound has bored into my brain. I begin howling. At night I dare not sleep. I fear the dreams. It is too terrible, the things that happen there. In my dream there is wind and blood moving as a stream. Red, dark blood in my dream. Rushing for our village. The blood moves faster. There are screams of wounded people. Animals are dead, thrown in the blood stream. There is nothing left. Only the air echoing nothing. Only the earth soaking up blood, spreading it in the four directions, becoming a thing there is no name for. I stand in the field watching the fire, The People watching me. We are waiting, but the answer is not clear yet. A crazy woman. That is what they call me.

1979

After taking a morning off work to see my lawyer, I come home, not caring if I call in. Not caring, for once, at the loss in pay. Not caring. My lawyer says there is nothing more we can do. I must wait. As if there has been something other than waiting. He has custody and calls the shots. We must wait and see how long it takes for him to get tired of being a mommy and a daddy. So, I wait.

I open the door to Patricia's room. Ellen and I keep it dusted and cleaned in case my baby will be allowed to visit us. The yellow and blue walls feel like a mockery. I walk to the windows, begin to systematically tear down the curtains. I slowly start to rip the cloth apart. I enjoy hearing the sounds of destruction. Faster, I tear the material into strips. What won't come apart with my hands, I pull at with my teeth. Looking for more to destroy, I gather the sheets and bedspread in my arms and wildly shred them to pieces. Grunting and sweating, I am pushed by rage and the searing wound in my soul. Like a wolf, caught in a trap, gnawing at her own leg to set herself free, I begin to beat my breasts to deaden the pain inside. A noise gathers in my throat and finds the way out. I begin a scream that turns to howling, then becomes hoarse choking. I want to take my fists, my strong fists, my brown fists, and smash the world until it bleeds. Bleeds! And all the judges in their flapping robes, and the fathers who look for revenge, are ground, ground into dust and disappear with the wind.

The word *lesbian*. Lesbian. The word that makes them panic, makes them afraid, makes them destroy children. The word that dares them. Lesbian. *I am one.* Even for Patricia, even for her, *I will not cease to be!* As I kneel amidst the colorful scraps, Raggedy Anns smiling up at me, my chest gives a sigh. My heart slows to its normal speech. I feel the blood pumping outward to my veins, carrying nourishment and life. I strip the room naked. I close the door.

Thanks so much to Chrystos for the title. Thanks to Gloria Anzaldúa for encouraging the writing of this story.

85

A Simple Act

for Denise Dorsz

Gourds climbing the fence. Against the rusted criss-cross wires, the leaves are fresh. The green, ruffled plants twine around the wood posts that need painting. The fruit of the vine hangs in irregular shapes. Some are smooth. Others bumpy and scarred. All are colors of the earth. Brown. Green. Gold

A gourd is a hollowed-out shell, used as a utensil. I imagine women together, sitting outside the tipis and lodges, carving and scooping. Creating bowls for food. Spoons for drinking water. A simple act—requiring lifetimes to learn. At times the pods were dried and rattles made to amuse babies. Or noisemakers, to call the spirits in sorrow and celebration.

I am taking a break from my hot room, from the writing, where I dredge for ghosts. The writing that unearths pain, old memories.

I cover myself with paper, the ink making tracks, like animals who follow the scent of water past unfamiliar ground.

I invent new from the old.

STORY ONE

Sandra

In the third, fourth, and fifth grades, we were best friends. Spending nights at each other's houses, our girl bodies hugging tight. We had much in common. Our families were large and sloppy. We occupied places of honor due to our fair skin and hair. Assimilation separated us from our ancient and inherited places of home. Your Russian gave way to English. Your blonde hair and freckles a counterpoint to the darkness of eye and black hair massed and trembling around your mother's head. My blonde hair, fine and thin, my skin pink and flushed in contrast to the sleek, black hair of my aunts, my uncle, my father. Their eyes dark, hidden by folds of skin. We were anachronisms . . . except to each other. Our friendship fit us well.

We invented stories about ourselves. We were children from another planet. We were girls from an undiscovered country. We were alien beings in families that were "different." Different among the different.

Your big sister Olga wore falsies. We stole a pair from her and took turns tucking them inside our undershirts. We pretended to be big girls, kissing on the lips and touching our foam rubber breasts. Imagining what being grown meant. In the sixth and seventh grades our blood started to flow, our breasts turned into a reality of sweet flesh and waiting nipples. The place between our thighs filled with a wanting so tender, an intensity of heat from which our fingers emerged, shimmering with liquid energy, our bodies spent with the expression of our growing strength. When we began to know what this was—that it was called love—someone told on us. Told on us. Through my bedroom window where we lay on the bed, listening to the radio, stroking blonde hair, Roger, the boy next door, saw us and told on us. Our mothers were properly upset. We heard the words from them: "You can't play with each other anymore." "You should be ashamed." "WHAT WILL PEOPLE THINK?"

We fought in our separate ways. You screamed in Russian as your father hit you with his belt. You cursed him, vowing revenge. Your mother watched, painfully, but did not interfere, upholding the morality of the family. My mother shamed me by promising not to tell the rest of the family. I refused to speak to her for weeks, taking refuge in silence, the acceptable solution. I hated her for the complicity we shared.

Sandra, we couldn't help but see each other. You lived across the street. We'd catch glimpses of the other running to school. Our eyes averted, never focusing. The belt marks, the silences, the shame, restoring us once again to our rightful places. We were good girls, nice girls, after all. So, like an old blouse that had become too thin and frayed, an embarrassment to wear, our friendship was put away, locked up inside our past. Entering the eighth grade in 1954, we were thirteen years old. Something hard, yet invisible, had formed over our memory. We went the way of boys, back seats of cars, self-destruction. I heard you were put in the hospital with sugar diabetes. I sent a card—unsigned. Your family moved away. I never saw you again.

Sandra, we are forty-one now.
I have three daughters.
A woman lover.
I am a writer.
Sandra, I am remembering our loss.
Sandra . . . I am remembering.
I loved you.

We have a basket filled with gourds. Our basket is woven from sweetgrass, and the scent stirs up the air and lights on our skin. This still life sits on a table in front of our bedroom window. In late afternoon, the sun glances around the hanging plants, printing designs on the wall and on our arms as we lay on our bed. We trust our love to each other's care. The room grows heavy with words. Our lungs expand to breathe the life gestating in the space connecting your eyes to mine. You put your hand on my face and imprint forever, in memory, this passage of love and faith. I watch you come from your bath. I pull you toward me, my hands soothed by the wetness on your back and between your thighs. You smell of cinnamon and clean water. Desire shapes us. Desire to touch with our hands, our eyes, our mouths, our minds. I bend over you, kissing the hollow of your throat, your pulse leaping under my lips.

We touch.

Dancers wearing shells of turtles, feathers of eagles, bones of our people.

We touch.

STORY TWO

My House

The house I grew up in was a small frame box. It had two stories. My sister, cousins, and I shared a room on the second floor. A chestnut tree rubbed its branches against our window. In the summer, we opened the glass panes and coaxed the arms of the tree into the room. Grandpa spoke to the tree every night. We listened to the words, holding our breath and our questions in fear of breaking a magic we knew was happening, but couldn't name.

In our house, we spoke the language of censure. Sentences stopped in the middle. The joke without a punch line. The mixture of a supposed-to-be-forgotten Mohawk, strangled with uneasy English.

I was a dreamer. I created places of freedom in my mind. Words that my family whispered in their sleep could be shouted. Words that we were not supposed to say could be sung, like the hymns Grandma sang on Sundays.

The secrets we held to ourselves. We swallowed them. They lay at the bottoms of our stomachs, making us fat with nerves and itching from inside.

The secrets we held to ourselves.

The secret that my mom's father refused to see her after she married a dark man, an Indian man.

The secret that my uncle drank himself to oblivion—then death.

The secret that Grandma didn't go out because storekeepers called her names—*dumb Indian, squaw.*

The secret that Grandpa carried a heart inside him clogged with the starches, the fats, the poverty of food that as a young boy, as an Indian, he had no choice about eating.

All of us, weighed down by invisible scales. Balancing always, our life among the assimilators and our life of memory.

We were shamed. We didn't fit. We didn't belong.
I had learned the lessons. I kept my mouth shut. I kept the quiet.

One night in August, 1954, a fire in the basement.
Things burned.
Secret things.
Indian things.
Things the neighbors never saw.
False Faces. Beaded necklaces. Old letters written in Mohawk. A
turtle rattle. Corn husks.
Secrets brought from home.
Secrets protecting us in hostile places.

"Did you lose anything?" The neighbors stood, anxious to not
know. The night air was hot. The moon hung full and white. The
stars in a crazy design over us.
"Did you lose anything?" The question came again.
"Just a few old things". . . and Grandma and Grandpa stepped
into the house, led by my mother's and father's hands. My grand-
parents tears were acid, tunneling holes in their cheeks.
"Don't forget this night, *kontirio*.* Don't forget this night."
Grandfather looked at me, the phrase repeated again and again.
"Don't forget this night."

Grandfather's back became a little more stooped. He lapsed into
Mohawk at odd moments. His heart stopped in his sleep. Heavy.
Constricted. Silenced.

Grandmother's back became a little thicker. Her shoulders were
two eagles transfixed on a mountain, checked in flight. Her hands

---

* wild animal

became large and knobby from arthritis. Still, she made the fry bread, the corn soup, the quilts, and changed the diapers of her great-grandchildren. She never spoke of that night. Her eyes faded, watery with age. She died. Her heart quitting in her sleep.

I closed the windows and covered my ears to the knocking of the tree.

In my room overlooking the back yard.
Through the open window, I smell the cut grass, hear the vines on the fence make a whispery sound. The gourds rattle as a breeze moves along quickly, bringing a promise of autumn and change.
I sit at the desk, pen in my hand, paper scattered underneath. Trying to bring forth sound and words.
Unblocking my throat.
Untying my tongue.
Scraping sand from my eyes.
Pulling each finger out of the fist I have carried at my side.
Unclenching my teeth.
Burning the brush ahead of me, brambles cutting across my mind.
Each memory a pain in the heart. But *this* heart keeps pumping blood through my body, keeping me alive.

I write because to not write is a breach of faith.

Out of a past where amnesia was the expected.
Out of a past occupied with quiet.
Out of a past, I make truth for a future.

Cultures gone up in flames.
The smell of burning leather, paper, flesh, filling the spaces where memory fails.
The smell of a chestnut tree, its leaves making magic.
The smell of Sandra's hair, like dark coffee and incense.

I close my eyes. Pictures unreeling on my eyelids.
Portraits of beloved people flashing by quickly.
Opening my eyes, I think of the seemingly ordinary things that women do. And how, with the brush of an eyelash against a cheek, the movement of pen on paper, power is born.

A gourd is a hollowed-out shell, used as a utensil.

We make our bowls from the stuff of nature. Of life.

We carve and scoop, discarding the pulp.

Ink on paper, picking up trails I left so many lives ago.

Leaving my mark, my footprints, my sign.

I write what I know.

Beth Brant (*Degonwadonti*) is a Bay of Quinte Mohawk from Theyindenaga reserve in Deseronto, Ontario. She was born May 6, 1941 in Grandma and Grandpa Brant's house in Detroit. According to her mother, it was the hottest day of the year, but Grandpa shoveled coal in the furnace and lit the fire, "just in case."

The author was married at seventeen and had three daughters—Kim, Jenny, and Jill. After she divorced, she attempted the job of raising her children on a high school drop-out's unskilled labor. She worked at various jobs: salesclerk, waitress, sweeper, cleaning woman, Title IV coordinator.

Brant began writing at the age of forty after a motor trip through the Mohawk Valley, where a Bald Eagle flew in front of her car, sat in a tree, and instructed her to write. She has been writing since.

She is co-founder of Turtle Grandmother, an archive and library of information about North American Indian women. Turtle Grandmother is also a clearinghouse for manuscripts, published and unpublished, by Indian women.

Brant belongs to the Turtle clan, as have all the women before her. She loves fry bread, corn soup, Heaven Hill bourbon, and being alive. She lives in Detroit with her lover of eight years, Denise, and two of her daughters.

Other titles from Firebrand Books include:

Jonestown & Other Madness, Poetry by Pat Parker
Moll Cutpurse, A Novel by Ellen Galford